This book is dedicated to all who find Nature not an adversary to conquer and destroy, but a storehouse of infinite knowledge and experience linking man to all things past and present. They know conserving the natural environment is essential to our future well-being.

DINOSAUR
THE STORY BEHIND THE SCENERY®

by Allen Hagood and Linda West

ALLEN HAGOOD, as a career professional of the National Park Service, lived and worked for many years at Dinosaur National Monument.

LINDA WEST now serves as a writer and illustrator for Dinosaur Nature Association, after several years as a ranger-naturalist at Dinosaur National Monument.

JEFF GNASS' spectacular land and aerial photography is featured in many of the scenic views for this book. He shares his appreciation of our national wonders through his camera.

Dinosaur National Monument located in northwestern Colorado and eastern Utah, was first set aside in 1915 to preserve the fossil remains of dinosaurs and other ancient animals.

Front cover: Camarasaurus skull on the quarry face, photo by Steve Mulligan. Inside front cover: The Green River flows around Steamboat Rock in Echo Park, photo by Jeff Gnass. Page 1: Working on a vertebrea, photo by Jeff Gnass. Pages 2/3: Whirlpool Canyon on the Green River, photo by Tom Till.

Edited by Mary L. Van Camp • Book design by K. C. DenDooven.

Tenth Printing, 2009 • New Version

DINOSAUR: THE STORY BEHIND THE SCENERY © 1990 KC PUBLICATIONS, INC.
LC 90-60037. ISBN 978-0-88714-041-9.

Ancient rocks are carved by the unrelenting force of running water. Today we see windows into past worlds.

The life that was the Dinosaur era
is well preserved for future study in
a place called Dinosaur National Monument

The Dinosaur Story

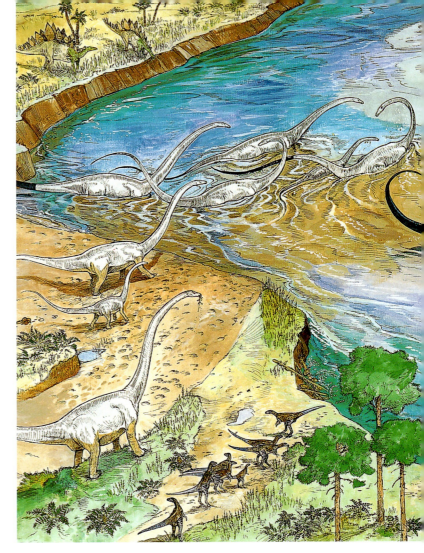

The land that is Dinosaur National Monument is far more than just the remains of ancient creatures. Here lies a story of a prehistoric river system that deposited its burden into collector areas where a unique series of events had to happen for us to witness the intense collection of dinosaur bones we can now visit at the quarry wall.

Dinosaur bones are not that uncommon throughout the world. What is special at this park is that here we have a concentrated collection of a large number of different dinosaurs. This area became a rich source of bones to the extent that museums all over the country exhibit the skeletons that came from the Dinosaur area.

Major John Wesley Powell, on his way to explore what is now the Grand Canyon, traversed the Green River that split Mountain Gorge in June/July 1869. He even named some of the features – Canyon of Lodore, Hell's Half Mile, Echo Rock, and Split Mountain Gorge.

Our first real explorers, settlers to the Dinosaur area goes back about 7,000 years, probably part of the migration story of humans coming across the Bering Strait from Asia into North America.

The Green and Yampa Rivers, which carved mountains, now serve as a liquid highway for river trips of all varieties. Float trips can be made on the Green – but the Yampa still rages forth to provide as exciting white river adventures as are called for anywhere.

K.C. DenDooven
Publisher

TOM DANIELSON

***At Dinosaur, and around the world, the search for** answers to our questions about dinosaurs goes on and, with every new find, new questions continue to challenge our intellect and imagination.*

***T**he painting above, which continues across* the next four pages, portrays many common events that probably took place at or near the quarry site 150 million years ago. At left, several large *Barosaurus* and three *Camptosaurus* (one of them threatened by crocodiles) are crossing the river. At right, two *Camarasaurus* keep a wary eye on a pair of Allosaurus feeding on a carcass. Other carcasses, bones, and tree trunks have been strewn by floodwaters on the riverbanks and sandbars; the next flood may bury some of them in sediments, thereby starting the process of fossilization.

***V**ertical sandstone flatirons along the* Island Park Fault attest to the inexorable forces of uplift. Formerly level like the strata in the background, the rocks were compressed and bend to the breaking point. Here they plunge downward along the fault, but level off again underground, hidden by younger strata in the foreground.

Out of the Rock

People of all races and nations have long pondered the ancient, unsolved riddle of life. But in few places does this philosophical enigma pervade the atmosphere more than it does at the Dinosaur Quarry of Dinosaur National Monument, in a remote corner of northeastern Utah. It hangs, an almost palpable question in the air, as the monument's thousands of visitors come face to face with the relics of an age that is almost incomprehensible in its antiquity—an age where reptilian giants and other singular beasts roamed a land that bore little resemblance to the rugged desert that now surrounds us.

The *first* impression upon entering the quarry, however, may be a simpler one—confusion! On a rock face before us is a jumble of fossil bones that looks like the leavings of an enormous turkey dinner. Many vertebrae in backbones are recognizable, and a few leg bones appear to be in correct juxtaposition. But nowhere in this puzzle of bone and rock do we see an entire and completely assembled dinosaur skeleton—the usual museum exhibit—as we had expected.

Instead, the quarry face exhibits only the bones, placed just as nature scattered them in the environment that existed here 150 million years ago, before the fossils were buried under tons and tons of river sand. Sure, at one time large loads of fossils from this area were removed and shipped to museums around the country, where they were painstakingly assembled into skeletons. Today, however, the fossil bones are not removed. Only about one-half of the rock that surrounds each bone was excavated. The fossils themselves were intentionally left in place on the hillside for exhibit and study. There they will remain, embedded in a tilted, 12-foot-thick layer that lies between other rock strata in the Morrison formation.

How did they get there? What did the animals to whom they once belonged look like? What kind of world existed then? How was this ancient boneyard finally discovered?

The answers to some of these questions—gained partly from the evidence, partly through scientific conjecture—are revealed in the bones themselves.

The individual dinosaurs whose bones are present here died from ordinary causes at varying times and places in or near an ancient river. Over a period of time this river carried some of the dead animals downstream. At certain places where the current became slower—in this case, on a sandbar in the river bend—the bloated bodies came to rest. As they lay there, the decaying carcasses were no doubt mauled and devoured by scavengers.

The bones were then scattered by the river currents, which deposited them here and there in mixed piles. It is even possible to determine the direction that the river flowed, simply by noting the position of some of the bones. The flexible body parts—the long tails and necks of some dinosaurs—trailed

JEFF GNASS

Monument paleontologists *now explore the Morrison formation outside of the quarry itself. Several sites have produced rare fossils of mammals and other small animals that lived along with the dinosaurs.*

downstream toward the east, where they came to lie and where they have been preserved to this day.

Only those bones that were completely covered by sand became fossilized. As soft parts—such as the marrow—decayed, silica filled the hollow spaces. As a result, the fossils are part rock (silica) and part actual dinosaur bone. The results of this process of preservation have often been so perfect that even the microscopic structure of the bone can now be seen in some specimens.

Tons of river sand accumulated upon the bones, followed by layers of volcanic ash and marine muds that compressed and formed rock that covered the fossils to a depth of about a mile. Then upheaval and erosion—occurring over millions of years—exhumed the ancient sandbar and its bountiful treasure.

This was the scenario in 1909, when scientist Earl Douglass came to search the Morrison formation in the hope of locating dinosaur fossils. How fortunate that erosion had at that particular time reached just the right level to expose the bones!

Douglass had been hired by Andrew Carnegie to find specimens for the then-new Carnegie Muse-

um in Pittsburgh. Knowing that remarkable dinosaur fossil finds had been made in the Morrison formation near Como Bluff, Wyoming, and Canon City, Colorado, Douglass hoped to make similar discoveries in that same formation but in the Uinta Basin, an area where only a few reptilian remains had previously been found.

On August 17, in a sandstone hogback at the present quarry site, Douglass discovered eight tail bones that belonged to Apatosaurus (Brontosaurus). Over the next 15 years, excavations by the Carnegie and other museums revealed finds that made this site one of the world's greatest sources of information about ancient life. Year after year the hard sandstone yielded its long-buried treasure to the scientists, until 350 tons—including 10 species of dinosaurs—had been shipped off to the museums. Most of these fossils went to the Carnegie Museum.

Carnegie officials, concerned about the possibility of losing the site to homesteaders or miners, strove for governmental protection of the quarry and its fossils. In 1915 an 80-acre area that contained the quarry site was declared a national monument, signed into law by President Woodrow Wilson.

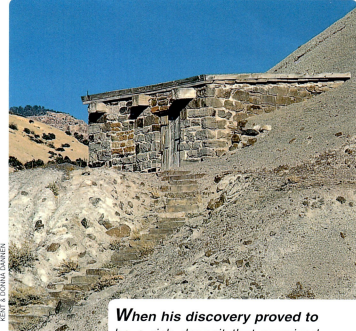

When his discovery proved to be a rich deposit that promised years of excavation, Earl Douglass built a house nearby, plus this small stone laboratory/ workshop that still stands behind the present quarry building.

Rock and fossil clues from many sites in the Morrison formation, in addition to the quarry itself, allow us to extend this scene beyond the ancient river. Sauropod trackways suggest that these animals traveled in herds, like the large group of *Diplodocus* on the preceding pages. Fossil wood indicates that tree ferns and tall pine-like *Araucaria* grew in many places; the sauropods (*Camarasaurus* and *Apatosaurus*, right foreground and rear) probably browsed on their foliage. *Stegosaurus* (left) and *Camptosaurus* (center foreground) ate lower-growing ferns and palm-like cycads.

Dinosaurs came in many shapes and sizes. *Apatosaurus*, though not the largest of them, was 70 feet long and weighed more than 30 tons. *Dryosaurus*, in contrast, was just 6 to 8 feet long and weighed about 150 pounds—some other dinosaurs were as small as chickens. *Stegosaurus*, mid-sized by dinosaur standards, was similar to a modern elephant in bulk (3 to 5 tons), but no living animal can match its odd bony plates and spikes.

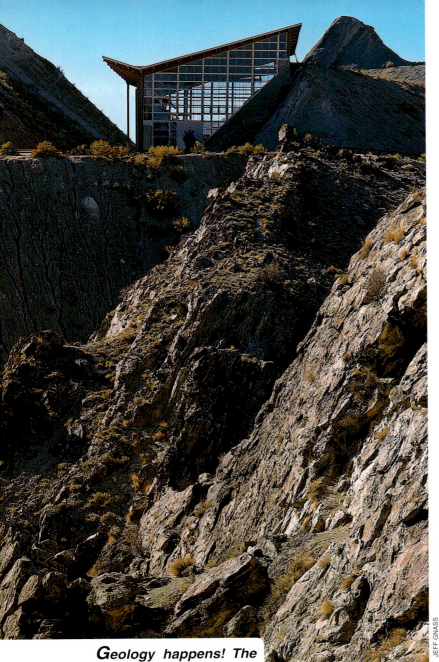

JEFF GNASS

Geology happens! *The earth does move. Due to unstable building conditions, the building enclosing the wall of fossilized bones has been closed. Visitors can still view fossil exhibits at the temporary visitor center and see fossil bone fragments by hiking a mile-long trail.*

Perhaps a CLUMSY "FRIEND" Stepped *on the* VICTIM'S *tail*

In the same year Douglass suggested that the government enclose the remaining fossils in a building to give them further protection. This would also provide a place for the public to view "one of the most astounding and instructive sights imaginable".

Douglass's idea was not implemented, until 1958, when a spacious, modern structure was built. It was constructed partly upon the sandstone ledge that Douglass had discovered nearly a half-century before. The building design embodies the National Park Service ideal of blending the works of man and nature into one harmonious whole.

Inside the quarry building, monument paleontologists have exposed more than 2,000 fossil bones in the rock face. Visitors can survey this unique exhibit from the lofty spectators' gallery, where it is easy to imagine that a play is about to begin on a stage 150 million years old.

The curtain rises on a vast plain containing many rivers. Mountains rise far to the west. They have been slowly eroding, and the eroded sand and mud are being carried in an easterly direction, toward the sea that covers the center of the continent.

The climate is warm and seasonally dry, and the prevailing vegetation, for the most part, is very strange. *Araucaria* "pines" (related to the present-day monkey puzzle trees of South America) tower up to 150 feet above the ground. About 50 feet below their tops are the crowns of ginkgos, tree ferns, and cycads. A verdant ground cover consists of small ferns, cycads, horsetails, fungi, and mosses. The world is a wilderness, in an age that is profoundly primeval.

Enter the principal player, the dominant land animal of the time—the dinosaur. Actually, many species of dinosaur are present, each living in its own habitat and in its own way, acting out a prehistoric drama. In our imagination we conjure up many versions of the dinosaur, "terrible lizard", for the very name fascinates us. Indeed, it is our fascination with these ancient and bizarre reptiles that acts as the magnet that draws many visitors to the monument. Exposed as we all have been to the fanciful distortions of the movies and the comic strips, we

A *life-sized model of* Stegosaurus **shows** one possible arrangement of the bony back plates: two rows, alternating from side to side. Since the plates were not directly attached to other bones, as fossils they are usually found scattered about, giving few or no clues to their exact position in life.

JEFF GNASS

are eager to ask questions about these remarkable animals. What about their true size, skin color, and appearance? What about their eggs, gizzard stones, and eating habits?

We cannot answer all of these questions, but we can draw a fairly good picture of the animals themselves. Shapes and sizes of the bones suggest how the various species used their bodies and fit into the larger scheme of nature.

For example, the gigantic sauropods—dinosaurs such as *Apatosaurus (Brontosaurus), Diplodocus,* and *Camarasaurus*—walked on all fours. We know this because their leg bones reveal adaptations for bearing great weight; also, the bones are similar to those of today's elephants.

Many paleontologists in the past described the sauropod dinosaurs as living almost exclusively in watery habitats. We now think that these long-necked, long-tailed creatures more likely spent most of their lives on land, sometimes traveling together in herds. Their long necks probably allowed them to browse in tall trees, in much the same manner as the giraffes of today.

Camptosaurus and *Dryosaurus* walked and ran on their hind legs, depending on speed to avoid predators. These smaller dinosaurs had teeth and horny beaks well suited to chewing the coarse vegetation of these times.

Stegosaurus was one of the strangest of all dinosaurs in appearance. This odd herbivore had a double row of plates down its back, four spikes on the end of its tail, and a small, beaked skull. Despite its bizarre looks, it must have been successful in its natural niche, for its fossilized bones are very common in the quarry.

What meat-eating dinosaurs have been found at the quarry? *Allosaurus* and *Ceratosaurus* were ferocious predators who walked on their hind legs. Strong claws, and gaping mouths filled with re-curved, serrated teeth leave little doubt about the general life pattern these dinosaurs followed. We do not specifically know whether these carnivores pursued their prey or were simply scavengers. As with modern carnivorous animals such as lions and ti-gers, they probably chose the young, sick, or old stragglers from among the smaller herbivores.

Most of the bones at the quarry belonged to plant-eating rather than flesh-eating dinosaurs. This ratio seems plausible, since it represents a situation commonly found in nature. In any life community, the energy provided by microorganisms and plant food passes first to the herbivores and then to the carnivores. The farther up the food chain, the fewer are the animals at each level.

Fossil turtles and crocodiles at the quarry—as well as many kinds of fossil mammals found at other sites both in the monument and elsewhere—indicate that other creatures interacted with the dinosaurs 150 million years ago. All these organisms were part of the Morrison environments and food chains, in relationships that were probably as complicated as any that exist on Earth today.

Some of the fossils at the Dinosaur Quarry suggest small incidents that make the dinosaurs' daily

continued on page 14

Inside the Quarry

Most of the quarry's fossil bones have been left in place in the rock as they were found, to create a unique exhibit and to preserve information (such as clues to the ways that the bones were transported and buried) that may be valuable to scientists. Fossils were removed, either because they lay in the outer part of the rock and concealed better specimens behind them, or because they were rare or unusual and deserved detailed study from all angles. The paleontologists take the fossils collected during summer field work into the quarry laboratory for cleaning, cataloging, and study. They also make molds and casts (exact replicas) of some specimens to lend to or exchange with other institutions. Much of this work is saved for winter when it is too cold to work at excavation sites away from the Dinosaur Quarry.

KENT & DONNA DANNEN

*E*ven for the short trip from quarry face to laboratory, the paleontologists wrap the fragile fossil bones in plaster-and-burlap jackets. Cracks in the sandstone often run through the bones as well, and the jacket helps support the bone and hold any broken pieces together. In the lab, the jacket protects the underside of the specimen while rock is cleaned from the surface.

*W*hether on the quarry face or in the lab, removing hard rock from breakable bones requires careful, patient work with fine tools such as small chisels and ice picks.

PHOTOGRAPHS BY KENT & DONNA DANNEN

*T*he tail spikes of *Stegosaurus* *were* presumably defensive, though they could have been used in territorial or mating battles.

Fossils of juvenile dinosaurs are usually rare, due to their smaller size and the incomplete bone development. However, the Dinosaur National Monument quarry has produced several juvenile dinosaur fossils, some of them the best specimens of their kind. Here a quarry paleontologist works on the vertebrae of a young *Diplodocus*.

JEFF GNASS

Peg-like teeth of *Diplodocus* may have "raked" foliage from tree branches.

KENT & DONNA DANNEN

Sharp, saw-edged teeth leave no doubt as to the diet of *Allosaurus*. New teeth, some of their points just visible in this partial jaw, constantly grew in to replace older ones that wore down or broke off.

JEFF GNASS

existence more real to us. This is true in the case of the tail of a *Camarasaurus*, in which two vertebrae were found fused together. Perhaps a clumsy "friend" stepped on the victim's tail, and the two injured bones gradually grew into one.

What else does the fossil record tell us about dinosaurian society? Baby dinosaurs, we are told, are rare in most fossil deposits—not so at the Dinosaur Quarry! A juvenile *Stegosaurus* and a few immature sauropods are present, indicating that several age groups existed here. This again reflects a situation that is usually found in nature. In many ways we find it is the ordinary rather than the extraordinary that emerges from the studies done at the quarry.

Even the quarry itself, as extraordinary as it is in the number and quality of its fossils, merely represents the natural ending of life for some individuals. It does not, as many people think, represent the extinction of the dinosaurs. The Morrison formation was deposited only halfway through the 150-million-year span in which the dinosaurs lived, and as a group they became even more successful in the later part of that span.

In this exhibit, lightweight replicas of a sauropod's hind leg bones have been assembled as they were arranged in life, showing the bones' massive structure and the straight, weight-supporting design of the joints. Behind the bones, the muscles have been reconstructed based on the shapes of the bones and on similar muscle patterns of living animals.

Sturdy, well-worn teeth in this lower jaw of *Camarasaurus* indicate that this dinosaur was not limited to a diet of "soft swamp plants," as was often stated in the past. More likely it browsed on the foliage of tree ferns and conifers.

PHOTOS BY KENT & DONNA DANNEN

The quarry also provides clues to other animals that lived with the dinosaurs, such as this turtle that is similar to today's pond turtles.

The dinosaurs, and certain other reptilian groups, disappeared rather rapidly some 80 million years after the time that the bones were deposited at the quarry. Dozens of explanations for their demise have been offered: climatic change, scarcity of food , mountain building, disease, competition from mammals (egg-eating or otherwise), volcanic eruptions, cosmic radiation, and over-specialization of the dinosaurs themselves. Yet there is no convincing evidence that overwhelmingly supports any one theory.

The unsolved mystery of dinosaurian extinction continues to be a hotly debated issue. The search for clues has confirmed the fact that throughout the history of life, extinction has been a natural and recurring process – always claiming a few species here and there, occasionally sweeping the planet in "great dyings" such as that which wiped out the dinosaurs and perhaps half of all species existing then.

Many people, gazing at the bones in the Dinosaur Quarry, feel a sense of loss that these fascinating beasts are gone forever. We can rebuild their skeletons, we can imagine their colors and sounds and movements, but we can never see a living, breathing *Diplodocus* or *Stegosaurus*. We cannot bring the dinosaurs back.

However, we can do something about the wave of extinctions now in progress, for unlike those of the past, we know the cause of this one. *We* are the cause!

In the cases of a few recently-extinct species, we know exactly when the last surviving individual was killed by humans. However, far more species – including many that we may never even have seen – have gone into oblivion not because of our direct hunting or harvesting, but because we have re-shaped so much of the Earth to suit ourselves.

Earth's habitats, both locally and globally, have always been changing, but usually slowly, allowing life to adapt to the change. When a forest is cut to the ground, a mountain is leveled by a strip mine, a desert is converted into a golf course – in a matter of days, months, or a few years, the native life cannot adapt. It must find the same kind of habitat elsewhere, or perish. Often there is nowhere else.

But there can be places like Dinosaur National Monument. The monument preserves more than a brief moment from the Age of Dinosaurs. Its rocks tell the story of nearly half of the Earth's long and eventful history, and of the slow changes of environments and life in the past. Its plateaus, canyons, and rivers are sanctuaries for today's life – habitats that we can try to protect from the too-rapid changes of the modern world, and species that we can try to pull back from the brink of extinction.

JEFF GNASS

Many of our ideas about dinosaurs have changed over the years, but one method of searching for clues remains the same: probing the rocks for their secrets.

SUGGESTED READING

LAMBERT, DAVID. *A Field Guide to Dinosaurs*. New York: Avon Books, 1983.

NORMAN, DR. DAVID. *The Illustrated Encyclopedia of Dinosaurs*. New York: Crescent Books, 1985.

OSTROM, JOHN H. *Dinosaurs*. Burlington, North Carolina: Carolina Biological Supply, 1984.

SATTLER, HELEN RONEY. *Dinosaurs of North America*. New York: Lothrop, Lee & Shepard Books, 1981.

WEST, LINDA, AND DAN CHURE. *Dinosaur: The Dinosaur National Monument Quarry*. Jensen, Utah: Dinosaur Nature Association, 1989.

*The close of the Age of Dinosaurs,
about 65 million years ago, was a
time of drastic change, marked in this
region by the uplift of the Rocky Mountains.*

A Rock-Leafed History

Fossils can be helpful clues in reading the
story of the rocks. The fossil of a brachiopod, a
clam-like animal, records one of many seas
that covered this area in the past.

The Age of Dinosaurs, remarkable as it was, is only
one small part of the story of the Earth that is told at
Dinosaur National Monument. The rocks themselves, if one knows how to read them, provide
chapters that far predate the dinosaur age in antiquity, and extend far beyond it to the very present.

The best place to begin reading this story is in
the Canyon of Lodore. Its towering, deep-red walls
are made of sand and pebbles eroded from an ancient mountain range that stood northeast of here.
The Dinosaur area itself was part of a long, steadily
sinking trough, slowly being filled in with the debris
of the eroding mountains. Compressed by their own
weight and cemented by hard silica, these sediments
became the rocks that we now call the Uinta Mountain group. They are estimated to be more than 1 *billion* years old.

If you float down the Green River through the
Canyon of Lodore, you can watch as these ancient
red rocks disappear below river level and are suc-
ceeded by thin-layered, light-brown rocks. This is
more than just a color change; it represents a break
of some half a billion years. During that time, an un-
known thickness of the Uinta Mountain group was
eroded away before a shallow sea gradually ad-
vanced over the area from the west and deposited
the thin, sandy layers now called the Lodore formation. There are other, smaller gaps in the record as
well, but overall, Dinosaur preserves the most extensive geologic history seen in any national park or
monument.

For some 300 million years or so, this area re-
mained fairly stable, often lying below sea level, and
rarely rising far above it. During almost all of this
time, seas, rivers, and wind dropped layer after layer
of mud, sand, silt, and pebbles – a vast pile of sediments some 9 miles thick. If you were to continue
floating down the Green River, you would eventually pass through all of these layers, though not exactly in order from the oldest to the youngest because later events have rearranged them in places.

Iron oxide coats most of the grains of rock in the
Uinta Mountain group, giving the strata their striking,
deep-red color. Firmly cemented with silica, the rocks
stand in near-vertical cliffs that tower more than 2,500
feet above the Green River in the Canyon of Lodore.

This aerial view of the Dinosaur Quarry and its surroundings spans many of the Mesozoic-era rocks found in the monument, from the older Glen Canyon Sandstone at right, representing desert dunes, to the younger beach and sea-floor sediments of the Frontier, Mowry, and Dakota layers at left. Mountain building tilted the strata, and erosion has exposed them in cross-section, etching valleys into softer layers, and leaving the harder ones standing in hogback ridges.

JEFF GNASS

Thus it helps to use a chart to stack the layers in their original order and read this part of the geological story in its proper sequence.

Life before, during, and after the time of the dinosaurs accounts for many lines in the story. Fossils of corals, crinoids, brachiopods, and mollusks mark the first great diversification of life in the ancient seas. Petrified wood and footprints of early reptiles record stages in the colonization of land. Dinosaur bones, seen in this context, simply portray one more of life's many adaptations to the constantly changing environments of the past.

The close of the Age of Dinosaurs, about 65 million years ago, was a time of drastic change, marked in this region by the uplift of the Rocky Mountains. This mountain building produced smaller ranges as well, including the Uinta Mountains which stretch across northeastern Utah and into the northwest corner of Colorado. Some peaks in the Uintas rise to more than 13,000 feet – but nearly 30,000 feet of rock has been worn away from above them.

This does not mean that the mountains origi-nally stood that much higher; instead, even as they first began to buckle upward, rain, snow, ice, and wind began to nibble away at them. Slowly but inexorably, this erosion stripped off layer after layer, finally exhuming the Uinta Mountain group from its long burial to form the backbone of the range. The younger rock layers, which had once been a continuous blanket above the Uinta Mountain group, are now exposed mainly in parallel bands along the flanks of the mountains.

Dinosaur National Monument lies near the eastern end of the Uintas, where the main uplift tapers off in a series of folds and faults. "Folding" may sound like something more readily done to a piece of paper than to solid rock, but with enough force and time, rock will bend. With too much bending, it will break; and if the blocks of rock on either side of a break move relative to one another, the break is called a fault.

Over a long time, folding and faulting can move rocks thousands of feet up, down, or sideways. You can see vivid examples at many places in Dinosaur, such as the great sweeping curve of the Mitten Park Fault below Harpers Corner and the steeply-tilted hogback ridges all around the Dinosaur Quarry.

Erosion has also been at work on these smaller bulges and bends, as it has on the broad arch of the main Uintas, stripping away many layers from the uplifted areas to expose the older rocks and leaving the younger rock layers more intact in the down-warped places. This is why the book of geological history here appears to have some of its pages bound in the wrong order. The layers that were once neatly stacked, oldest on the bottom and youngest on the top, have been bent, tilted, and carved into a complex landscape – one that can be as challenging to understand as it is to walk through.

Perhaps the greatest challenge is in reading the latest chapter of the geological story. The chief characters in this chapter are the Green and Yampa rivers, and in their courses across Dinosaur, they seem to defy logic.

Where the Yampa River enters the monument at Deerlodge Park, it flows in an open valley eroded in relatively soft rock. Then, however, it plunges into its canyon by cutting across older, harder rocks that are tilted downward to the east—directly against the view's westward flow. The Green River makes an

The Uinta Mountain group cliffs in the Canyon of Lodore, and here in the small side canyon called Winnie's Grotto, are actually only a small part of this rock formation. Its total thickness of some 24,000 feet represents an immensely long time of sedimentation that began more than a billion years ago.

TOM TILL

POWELL *theorized* "the River HAD *the* RIGHT of way"

even more dramatic entrance at the Gates of Lodore, leaving an apparently easy course down the valley of Browns Park and boring directly into the 2,000-foot-high ramparts of the Uinta Mountain group. In the next 40-odd miles the river crosses several faults—often from the *down*dropped side to the *up*lifted side—and for a grand finale slices right through the center of a dome-shaped fold (the aptly named Split Mountain).

When John Wesley Powell explored the Green River in 1869, he theorized that "the river had the right of way." In other words, that it , and also the Yampa, were already flowing in their present courses on fairly level ground before the folding and faulting began. Then, as the uplift slowly proceeded,

Sculpting a Landscape a "Time-lapse" Overview

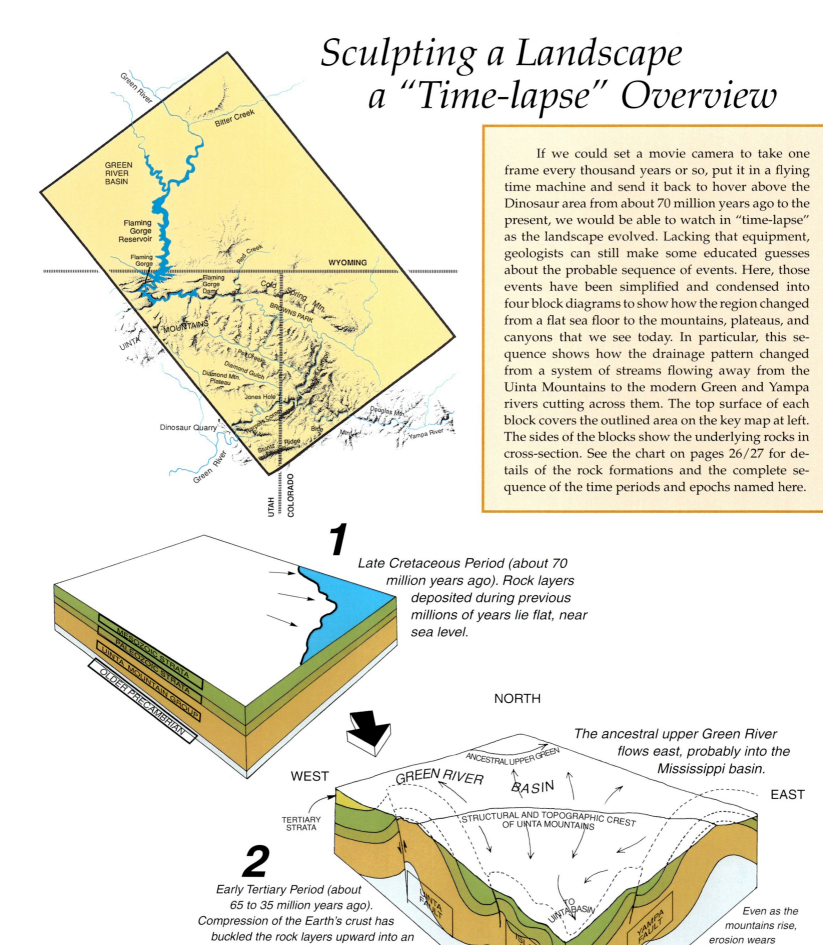

If we could set a movie camera to take one frame every thousand years or so, put it in a flying time machine and send it back to hover above the Dinosaur area from about 70 million years ago to the present, we would be able to watch in "time-lapse" as the landscape evolved. Lacking that equipment, geologists can still make some educated guesses about the probable sequence of events. Here, those events have been simplified and condensed into four block diagrams to show how the region changed from a flat sea floor to the mountains, plateaus, and canyons that we see today. In particular, this sequence shows how the drainage pattern changed from a system of streams flowing away from the Uinta Mountains to the modern Green and Yampa rivers cutting across them. The top surface of each block covers the outlined area on the key map at left. The sides of the blocks show the underlying rocks in cross-section. See the chart on pages 26/27 for details of the rock formations and the complete sequence of the time periods and epochs named here.

1 Late Cretaceous Period (about 70 million years ago). Rock layers deposited during previous millions of years lie flat, near sea level.

NORTH

WEST

EAST

2 Early Tertiary Period (about 65 to 35 million years ago). Compression of the Earth's crust has buckled the rock layers upward into an irregular arch shape—the Uinta Mountains and some smaller folds. Where the rocks were bend too steeply, they broke and slipped farther along faults (only major faults are shown).

The ancestral upper Green River flows east, probably into the Mississippi basin.

Even as the mountains rise, erosion wears them down, stripping off thousands of feet of rock (dotted lines) from the summits. Much of the eroded material is redeposited in the basins at the feet of the mountains.

SOUTH

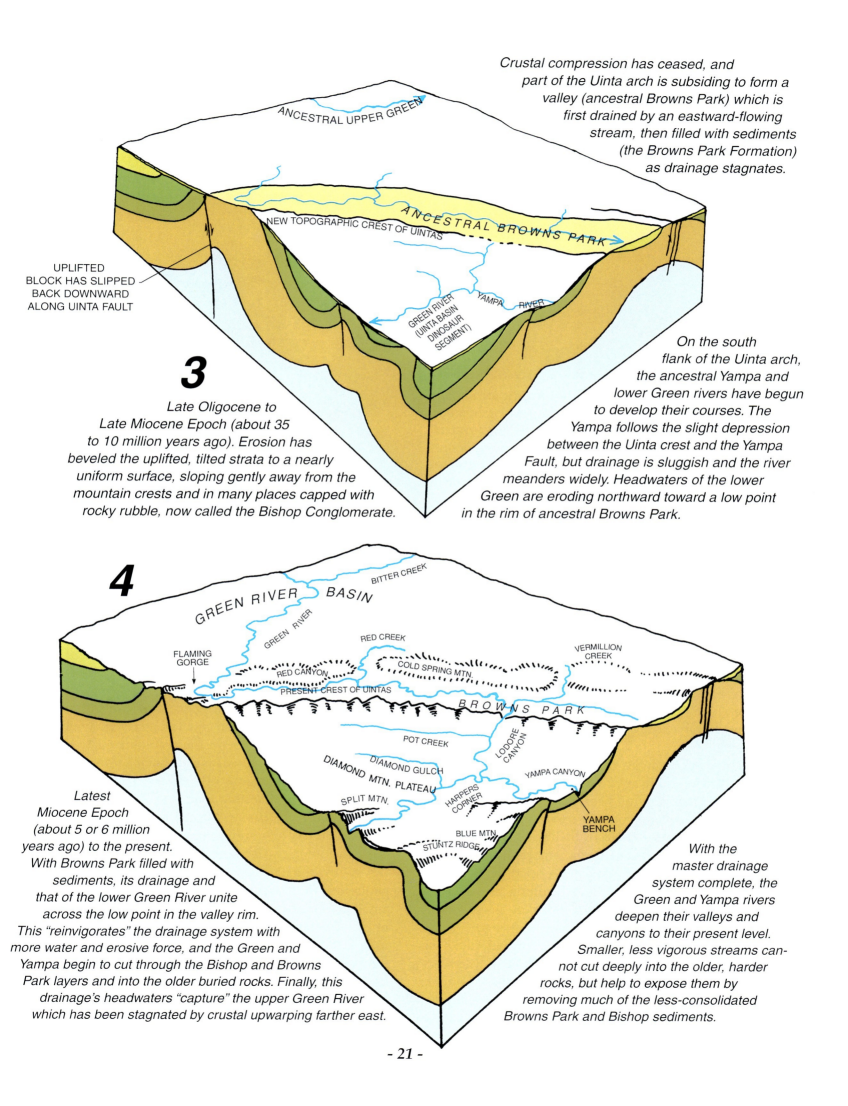

3

ANCESTRAL UPPER GREEN

NEW TOPOGRAPHIC CREST OF UINTAS

ANCESTRAL BROWNS PARK

UPLIFTED BLOCK HAS SLIPPED BACK DOWNWARD ALONG UINTA FAULT

GREEN RIVER (UINTA BASIN DINOSAUR SEGMENT)

YAMPA RIVER

Crustal compression has ceased, and part of the Uinta arch is subsiding to form a valley (ancestral Browns Park) which is first drained by an eastward-flowing stream, then filled with sediments (the Browns Park Formation) as drainage stagnates.

Late Oligocene to Late Miocene Epoch (about 35 to 10 million years ago). Erosion has beveled the uplifted, tilted strata to a nearly uniform surface, sloping gently away from the mountain crests and in many places capped with rocky rubble, now called the Bishop Conglomerate.

On the south flank of the Uinta arch, the ancestral Yampa and lower Green rivers have begun to develop their courses. The Yampa follows the slight depression between the Uinta crest and the Yampa Fault, but drainage is sluggish and the river meanders widely. Headwaters of the lower Green are eroding northward toward a low point in the rim of ancestral Browns Park.

4

GREEN RIVER BASIN

BITTER CREEK

GREEN RIVER

RED CREEK

VERMILLION CREEK

FLAMING GORGE

RED CANYON

COLD SPRING MTN.

PRESENT CREST OF UINTAS

BROWNS PARK

POT CREEK

LODORE CANYON

DIAMOND GULCH

DIAMOND MTN. PLATEAU

HARPERS CORNER

YAMPA CANYON

SPLIT MTN.

YAMPA BENCH

BLUE MTN.

STUNTZ RIDGE

Latest Miocene Epoch (about 5 or 6 million years ago) to the present. With Browns Park filled with sediments, its drainage and that of the lower Green River unite across the low point in the valley rim. This "reinvigorates" the drainage system with more water and erosive force, and the Green and Yampa begin to cut through the Bishop and Browns Park layers and into the older buried rocks. Finally, this drainage's headwaters "capture" the upper Green River which has been stagnated by crustal upwarping farther east.

With the master drainage system complete, the Green and Yampa rivers deepen their valleys and canyons to their present level. Smaller, less vigorous streams cannot cut deeply into the older, harder rocks, but help to expose them by removing much of the less-consolidated Browns Park and Bishop sediments.

Above, the phosphate-rich Park City formation *supports a blanket of junipers between two intermittent drainages that have cut into the underlying Weber Sandstone on the flanks of Split Mountain. A spring-fed stream has cut more deeply into the sandstone to form a box canyon. These "consequent streams," whose courses are determined by the strata's tilt, flow more or less straight down the slopes in contrast to the Green and Yampa rivers that cut across the uplifts.*

the rivers cut downward at the same pace, like a power saw cutting through a log being pushed up against it.

There is, alas, a flaw in this elegantly simple explanation: the uplift began about 65 million years ago, but the rivers are not nearly that old. We know this because of several younger rock layers made of sediments that were eroded from the rising Uinta Mountains and redeposited in the adjacent basin. These layers, which could not have formed as they are if the rivers had already been draining those basins, preclude the rivers having been in their present courses until about 5 or 6 million years ago.

These same layers, however, provide the basis for the currently-preferred explanation of the rivers' development. This theory holds that these younger sediments virtually buried all but the highest peaks and ridges of the eastern Uintas, filling in valleys

such as Browns Park and concealing the various faults and folds. The Green and Yampa rivers, which developed their courses on the resultant relatively even surface, began to cut fairly easily through the soft young sediments and then were "trapped" in those courses by the time renewed uplifting of the region occurred. This revitalized the rivers, and as they began to erode more vigorously, they encountered the older, harder, bent, and tilted rocks.

With their courses already set, the rivers had no choice but to cut through those rocks as well. Their smaller, less powerful tributaries meanwhile eroded only the softer young sediments, revealing the structure of the older buried rocks. Thus Split Mountain, for instance, had already been a "whole" mountain; it was buried by the younger sediments, cut through by the Green River, and re-exposed as the younger sediments were eroded from its top and sides.

Erosion is still etching the landscape and deepening the canyons, though we rarely notice it except in sudden, "catastrophic" events. Such an event occurred on June 10, 1965, when unusually heavy rains sent tons of water, soil, and boulders down a draw and into the Yampa River. This debris slurry dammed the river for several hours until it rose and spilled over the barrier, sweeping away the finer sediments but leaving huge blocks of rock that formed Warm Springs Rapid.

Had certain other events been different, that flash flood might have been swallowed almost unnoticed in the waters of a man-made reservoir. We, too, have become a geological force, able to carve a landscape or control a river's flow to suit our own purposes, but in Dinosaur National Monument we have chosen, for the present at least, to limit our powers. We have indeed had an impact on the land, water, and life here, but we can measure our own effects against an unparalleled record of natural changes, both past and present. Perhaps the comparison will inspire us to be more careful in the choices and changes we make in the future.

SUGGESTED READING

HANSEN, WALLACE R. *The Geologic Story of the Uinta Mountains.* Washington, D.C.: U.S. Geological Survey, 1969.

HAYES, PHILIP T., and GEORGE C. SIMMONS. *River Runners' Guide to Dinosaur National Monument and Vicinity.* Denver: Powell Society, Ltd., 1973.

JEFF GNASS

At Rainbow Park, the Green River leaves a seemingly logical path in soft strata and cuts directly across tilted layers into the center of Split Mountain. When the river developed this course, however, the mountain was buried by younger sediments and the valley around it did not exist.

Overleaf: Briefly free from hard, confining rocks, the Green River meanders lazily through Island Park. Photo by Jeff Gnass.

A Slice of Rocks and Time

Drawn like a giant slice through the Uinta Mountains and Basin, this chart summarizes Dinosaur's complex geological history. The rock formations vary much more in thickness than can be shown here, but they are in their proper order, from oldest at left to youngest at right, and are tilted in much the same way as they appear in most of the area. The geologic time line along the bottom shows the eras and periods in which the formations were deposited, as well as the gaps (black areas) in the record—times when no rocks were deposited, or those that had been were eroded away. The circled numbers at the right end match those in the diagrams on pages 20/21 to show the approximate times during which the events in the diagrams took place.

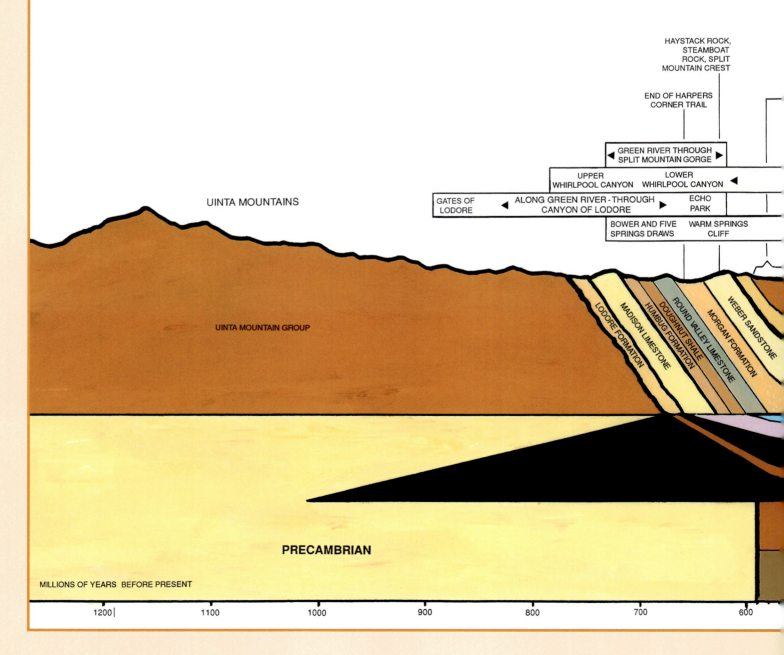

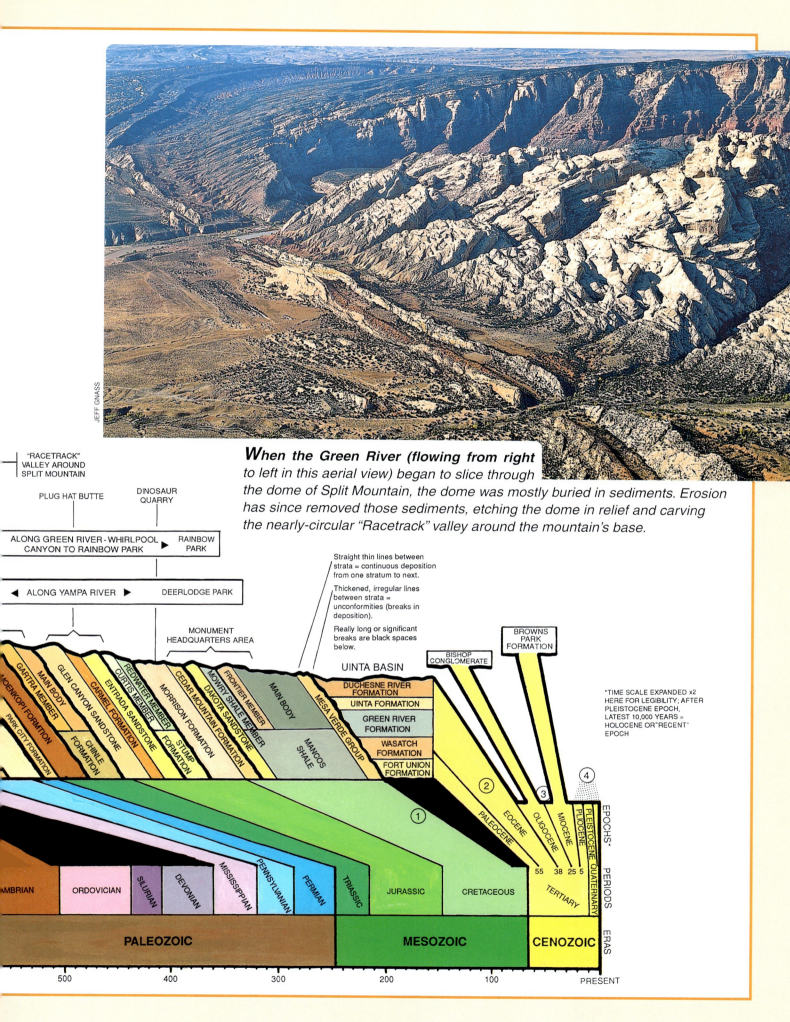

JEFF GNASS

When the Green River (flowing from right to left in this aerial view) began to slice through the dome of Split Mountain, the dome was mostly buried in sediments. Erosion has since removed those sediments, etching the dome in relief and carving the nearly-circular "Racetrack" valley around the mountain's base.

"RACETRACK" VALLEY AROUND SPLIT MOUNTAIN

PLUG HAT BUTTE

DINOSAUR QUARRY

ALONG GREEN RIVER - WHIRLPOOL CANYON TO RAINBOW PARK ► RAINBOW PARK

◄ ALONG YAMPA RIVER ► DEERLODGE PARK

MONUMENT HEADQUARTERS AREA

Straight thin lines between strata = continuous deposition from one stratum to next.

Thickened, irregular lines between strata = unconformities (breaks in deposition).

Really long or significant breaks are black spaces below.

UINTA BASIN

BISHOP CONGLOMERATE

BROWNS PARK FORMATION

*TIME SCALE EXPANDED x2 HERE FOR LEGIBILITY; AFTER PLEISTOCENE EPOCH, LATEST 10,000 YEARS = HOLOCENE OR "RECENT" EPOCH

PARK CITY FORMATION · MOENKOPI FORMATION · GARTRA MEMBER · MAIN BODY · CHINLE FORMATION · GLEN CANYON SANDSTONE · CARMEL FORMATION · ENTRADA SANDSTONE · REDWATER MEMBER · CURTIS FORMATION · MORRISON FORMATION · STUMP FORMATION · CEDAR MOUNTAIN FORMATION · DAKOTA SANDSTONE · MOWRY SHALE MEMBER · FRONTIER MEMBER · MAIN BODY · MESA VERDE GROUP · MANCOS SHALE

DUCHESNE RIVER FORMATION
UINTA FORMATION
GREEN RIVER FORMATION
WASATCH FORMATION
FORT UNION FORMATION

① ② ③ ④

PALEOCENE · EOCENE · OLIGOCENE · MIOCENE · PLIOCENE · PLEISTOCENE

EPOCHS*

55 · 38 · 25 · 5

CAMBRIAN · ORDOVICIAN · SILURIAN · DEVONIAN · MISSISSIPPIAN · PENNSYLVANIAN · PERMIAN · TRIASSIC · JURASSIC · CRETACEOUS · TERTIARY · QUATERNARY

PERIODS

PALEOZOIC · **MESOZOIC** · **CENOZOIC**

ERAS

500 · 400 · 300 · 200 · 100 · PRESENT

*O*verall, life in Dinosaur today
seems to be far more diverse than at
any single time in the geologic past.

More Than Dinosaurs,
and More Than Desert

Some plants have such strict needs that they will grow only on certain rock formations. The "desert trumpet," a species of wild buckwheat, favors clayey soils derived from the Mowry Shale.

When snow and spring rains have been sufficient, flowers such as Rocky Mountain bee plant erupt in displays that rival the colors in the rocks.

LINDA WEST

TOM TILL

Dinosaur National Monument seems to resist classifications. It is named for dinosaurs, but most of its 330-square-mile area has nothing to do with them. Its rock strata are characteristic of the Colorado Plateau, but their folding and faulting ties the area into the geologic structure of the Rocky Mountains. Climatically and biologically, the monument is part of the Great Basin Desert, but its weather, plants, and animals are much more diverse than "desert" suggests.

Heat may first come to mind when you think of a desert, and indeed summer temperatures in parts of Dinosaur can top 100° F, but in the winter the mercury can drop to 30 or 40° below zero. This is a cold desert, characterized by winter snow as well as summer heat. What actually makes it a desert or semi-desert is dryness: average annual precipitation here, varying with altitude, is only about 9 to perhaps 20 inches. These figures include the meager water content of the snow as well as rain, much of which falls in brief, localized cloudbursts that may send a flash flood down one canyon while leaving another bone-dry.

Dinosaur's elevation ranges from about 4,740 feet along the Green River as it leaves the monument to 9,006-foot Zenobia Peak on the highlands between Lodore and the Yampa. Along with this range of altitudes, the rugged and varied terrain creates many micro-climates. In deep, narrow gorges, under cliff overhangs, or simply on northern-facing slopes and canyon walls, sunlight penetrates less and moisture lingers a bit longer. Such places can harbor tall Douglas firs or hanging gardens of ferns and mosses, while cacti or yuccas grow on open dry ledges just a few feet away.

Abundant water, in certain places, further belies the "desert" description. The Green and Yampa rivers bring the melted snows from the Wind River Range of Wyoming and the Rockies of Colorado, respectively, into the rock-ribbed canyons. Few fish could survive in the original conditions of these rivers—wildly varying seasonal flows, warm summer water temperatures, and heavy sediment loads—but some fish did adapt, giving rise to several endemic species, native to this region and found nowhere else in the world.

A few smaller streams such as Jones Hole Creek originate from springs where groundwater, slowly traveling down from higher elevations through porous sandstone or limestone, reaches the surface. Usually clearer than the main rivers, these streams host a great variety of small aquatic life, including algae, plankton, insects, and other invertebrates. These are the base of the food chain that extends on

NPS PHOTO BY DAVID WHITMAN

Ancient people hunted the native bighorn sheep, and often pictured it in their rock art. Modern people extirpated the bighorn, reintroduced it, and are sometimes lucky enough to capture it on film.

up to fishes in both the creeks and the main rivers, and out of the water as well—to mink and river otters, great blue herons and bald eagles.

Further, all of these watercourses, both large and small, form linear oases through the monument. Shaded by broad-leafed trees such as cottonwood and box elder, they are home to beaver, dippers, Canada geese, and other wildlife not usually found in a desert.

Even away from the rivers and washes, Dinosaur's landscape is no barren wasteland. The higher peaks and canyon rims support stands of ponderosa pine and Douglas fir, grading into pinyon-juniper woodland at the middle elevations and on down into sagebrush, greasewood, and other desert or semi-desert shrubs. These are simply the dominant plants; all are parts of complex communities that include characteristic associations of various trees, shrubs, herbs, and grasses.

GRAZING

took its TOLL

on **Plant** Life

AS *well*

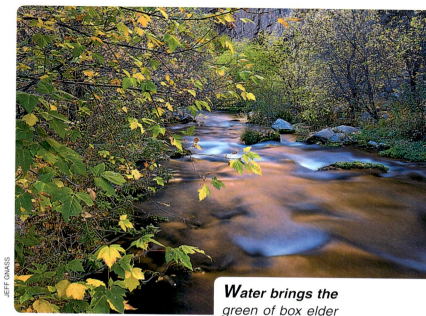

JEFF GNASS

Water brings the green of box elder leaves to Jones Hole, and frost brings the first hint of autumn gold. Both water and frost add to the diversity of land and life here.

NPS PHOTO BY DAVID WHITMAN

Canada geese usually nest on islands, but in the Canyon of Lodore they have adapted to rocky ledges above the water—an advantage on the fluctuating dam—controlled Green River.

Most of these plants can withstand dryness, and some, such as greasewood and saltbush, can also tolerate the salty or alkaline soils that occur in much of the area. Some soils, derived from shaly strata such as the Moenkopi, Chinle, and Morrison, may contain the toxic element selenium, yet several species of plants have developed the ability to absorb it without harm and grow only on those formations.

Such adaptations to special conditions, combined with the natural geographic barrier of the canyons and mountain ranges, have given Dinosaur and the surrounding region a tremendous diversity of plants, with an unusually high proportion of endemic species. Within the monument alone, some 550 different plant species have been identified, and researchers estimate that another 200 to 250 will be found if the area is fully studied.

Each community also has its typical animal members, ranging from mule deer, coyotes, and mountain lions to jackrabbits, lizards, and snakes. Many of the larger mammals range widely and may frequent both arid and riparian (riverside) areas, but most rely on the rivers, streams, and springs for drinking water. In contrast, many of the reptiles and smaller mammals are well-adapted to arid places, with physiologies that conserve water or can even produce it metabolically from dry foods.

Overall, life in Dinosaur today seems to be far more diverse than at any single time in the geologic past. Many environments, and many kinds of plants and animals, have come and gone through the ages, but never until this particular geologic moment have so many different habitats and life forms existed together within this relatively small area. And never until this particular geologic moment has one single life form had such power to change, even destroy, that diversity.

THE BEGINNINGS OF CHANGE

Even now, the life we see in Dinosaur is not the same as it was only a century or two ago. In 1825, William Ashley wrote in his journal that he saw "about 100 Buffalloe [*sic*]" and "great abundance of Elk" in Island Park. George Bradley, a member of Powell's 1869 expedition, lost several hooks and lines to Colorado squawfish, "great fellows some of them quite a yard long," before landing one in Echo

Park. One of the most striking photographs taken on Powell's second expedition, just inside the Gates of Lodore, shows a smooth sandy beach beside the river.

Yet even as they recorded what they saw, these people marked the beginnings of change. Ashley's men and other trappers in the heyday of the fur trade nearly wiped out the beaver. It has since recovered, but the river otter, never as abundant as beaver to begin with, has not and is now rarely seen in Dinosaur's waters.

Permanent settlement, even as sparse as it was, had a more profound and widespread impact on the Dinosaur region. Settlers brought in cattle and sheep, which competed with the native animals for forage and sometimes infected them with parasites and disease. Along with hunting, this displaced or reduced many wildlife populations, and totally eliminated bison, grizzly bears, and bighorn sheep from the area.

Grazing took its toll on plant life as well. As livestock ate the native grasses, sagebrush often spread into the former grassland. Unpalatable exotic plants (such as cheatgrass and Russian thistle) which had been accidentally introduced in seed or grain shipments also proliferated in place of the native species.

C. ALLAN MORGAN

The porcupine's preferred diet, the soft inner bark of trees, serves it well in the winter when other foods are scarce. Having few natural enemies, porcupines could potentially destroy a forest, but a low reproductive rate counterbalances their efficient defenses.

The tamarisk's feathery purple blooms made it a popular ornamental shrub—until it escaped from cultivation and spread through the entire Colorado River Basin, often choking out the native plants of the riverbanks.

NPS PHOTO

Water development, ultimately on a far greater scale than Powell ever imagined, brought still more change in the form of Flaming Gorge and numerous other dams. Of the six fish species endemic to the Colorado River and its tributaries, four—the Colorado squawfish, humpback and bonytail chubs, and razorback sucker—are now endangered. Adapted to muddy, sun-warmed, turbulent rivers, they cannot reproduce in deep, still reservoirs, nor in the cold, clear, controlled tailwaters that may extend many miles below the dams. Moreover, introduced fishes—many of them favored by the reservoir and tailwater conditions—compete with or prey upon the native species.

The beach in the 1871 Powell photograph is now hidden by a dense thicket, mostly of tamarisk. This exotic shrub escaped from cultivation in the Southwest and spread throughout the Colorado

Sinking their roots into cracks in the sandstone, Douglas firs cling to a cliff above Jones Hole. The north-facing canyon wall provides the slightly cooler, moister habitat that the trees need.

River Basin. The lack of natural floods that used to scour out many of its seedlings has aided the tamarisk's invasion of the riverbanks. This, in turn, has resulted in loss of habitat for both native plants and wildlife.

THE PRESERVATION COMMITMENT

Despite such changes, Dinosaur National Monument still affords a rare opportunity to preserve the natural diversity that is vanishing from much of our world. The original proclamation of the Dinosaur Quarry as a national monument was just the start of a preservation commitment that was broadened in the monument expansion, and tested and strengthened in the battle over the Echo Park and Split Mountain dams.

That commitment has also evolved along with our understanding of natural processes. For many years, for instance, it was widely believed that fire should be fought whenever it occurred. Few people stopped to consider that in a climate where dry thunderstorms are common, lightning-caused fires must also have been common for ages before anyone was here to put them out.

Now we realize that natural fires help to maintain a mosaic of varied plant communities, clearing out shrubs and trees here and there and allowing grasses to grow, in turn creating diverse habitats for varied wildlife. Several decades of fire suppression, combined with the effects of more than a century of grazing, had reduced that diversity of wildlife.

Dinosaur's resource management program is, ultimately, an effort to restore diversity and to maintain it by allowing natural processes to operate. One aspect of this is the gradual phase out of grazing from monument lands. Another is the restoration of fire to its natural ecological role.

The monument's fire management plan is not a "let-burn" policy, but it spells out conditions and objectives for the use of fire, both naturally-ignited and set by resource managers. In many cases, fire can help to speed the recovery of overgrazed land by clearing out sagebrush and stimulating regrowth of native grasses.

Much wildlife is already benefiting from the removal of grazing and restoration of fire. Elk, for instance, have migrated into the protected monument from adjacent lands that are open to hunting and have become increasingly common because of the improved forage they find. Other animals that had been locally extirpated need more help, and reintroducing them is another step in restoring Dinosaur's diversity.

Archaeological sites, rock art, and historical accounts all show that bighorn sheep once roamed throughout Dinosaur's canyon country. They began to die off sharply in the 1930s and were officially declared extirpated from the monument in 1951. The most likely cause of this rapid decline was grazing by domestic sheep, which both reduced the forage and carried parasites and diseases to which the bighorns had no resistance.

In 1952, the Colorado state wildlife agency released a small herd of bighorns just outside the Canyon of Lodore. Moving into the canyon, the herd multiplied from 32 to about 150 animals, but then, after several years, the population began to decline again. This time inbreeding, which may have made the animals more susceptible to disease and stress, was suspected as the major problem. So in 1984 another bighorn herd, genetically distinct, was transplanted on the benchlands below Harpers Corner. It

NPS PHOTO

A *downy peregrine falcon chick (above) receives a leg band that will identify it wherever it travels as an adult (left). Nearly wiped out by pesticide poisoning, peregrine falcons are making a comeback, thanks to intensive recovery efforts in Dinosaur and elsewhere. However, their future is still very much in our hands.*

is hoped that these animals will interbreed with the Lodore herd, strengthening both populations.

However, bighorns are poor pioneers—they are reluctant to migrate, even into parts of their former range, especially through tall, dense shrubs such as the sagebrush that has proliferated due to fire suppression and grazing. Thus the success of bighorn reintroduction depends on the whole resource management effort—restoring not just the animals themselves, but the *habitat* they need for a self-sustaining population.

The same is true for all wildlife. We cannot simply "protect" certain animals; we must also preserve the ecosystem of which they are a part. For some animals, Dinosaur may be the only place where we even have a chance to do so.

LAST CHANCE FOR THE FISHES?

Three of the four rare endemic fishes still live in the rivers in Dinosaur. The reason for their survival here is the Yampa River—the last relatively free-flowing river in the entire Colorado River System.

The lower Yampa harbors a "pure" population of humpback chubs. Elsewhere in the Upper Basin (the portion of the Colorado and its tributaries upstream from Lees Ferry, Arizona), these fish have hybridized with the more common roundtail chub due to dam-caused changes that forced the two species to share limited habitat.

The Colorado squawfish, whose lengthy spawning migrations (now mostly blocked by dams) earned it the nickname of "Colorado salmon," now spawns at only two known sites. One of them is on the Yampa in Dinosaur, the other in Desolation Canyon on the Green River more than 100 miles below the mouth of the Yampa (but, even at that distance, with more natural flows thanks to the Yampa). Above the Yampa, the Green no longer offers the high spring/low summer flows, particular type of cobble bottom, and quiet backwater "nursery" areas (which may be 50 to 75 miles downriver from the spawning sites) that the squawfish and their fry need.

Razorback suckers likewise live in the lowermost Yampa and in the Green below the confluence. Ironically, though the razorbacks spawn prolifically, virtually all specimens caught for study appear to be *older* than Flaming Gorge Dam—their fry have not survived to replenish the population since the dam's completion. Predation by introduced fishes is suspect of wiping out the fry, so biologists are attempting to raise young razorbacks in predator-free ponds until they are large enough to survive in the rivers.

Similar efforts may be the only hope for the rarest of the native fishes, the bonytail chub. It has probably already been extirpated from the rivers in Dinosaur, and most of the few known individuals elsewhere have been caught for breeding and rearing in hatcheries. Some of these captive-bred bony-tails have been released for study in the monument, and their fate may tell us what the future holds for this species. The future for all rare fishes depends not only on our direct help, but on preserving their habitat—the free-flowing Yampa River, undammed not only within Dinosaur National Monument but upstream as well.

RETURN OF THE PEREGRINES

We do know that suitable habitat plus human help can make a difference for an endangered species. Certain birds that return to Dinosaur's canyons each spring are proof, for they are also returning from the verge of extinction.

The peregrine falcon eats other birds, which it catches mid-air in spectacular dives that may reach speeds close to 200 miles an hour. Unfortunately, many of those meals have been seasoned with toxic by-products of DDT and other pesticides. One small bird may not carry much pesticide residue, but each peregrine eats many small birds, thus concentrating the poison in its body.

This causes the falcon to lay abnormally thin-shelled eggs, which either break under the weight of the brooding parents or lose so much moisture that the embryos die before they can hatch. Formerly breeding all across North America, the peregrine disappeared from east of the Rockies in the 1950s and '60s , and by the late 1970s occupied only a few known aeries (nests) in the West.

One of those aeries was in Dinosaur, and so the monument became a participant in a peregrine recovery program that is still going on. Each spring, biologists, park rangers, and volunteers watch for returning peregrines, note their aerie sites, and record when and if they lay eggs (usually 3 or 4 to a clutch). If the aerie is accessible (which may mean by rappelling off a 1,000-foot cliff) the eggs are removed 7 to 10 days after laying and taken to the World Center for Birds of Prey in Boise, Idaho, where they are incubated under controlled conditions to increase their chance of hatching.

Meanwhile, the parent birds are "incubating" dummy eggs that were left in place of the real ones. A few days before the normal incubation period ends, the dummy eggs are in turn replaced with live chicks, raised in captivity until they are about three weeks old and hardy enough to have a high chance of survival. This sudden "hatching" surprises the foster parents, but instinct soon takes over, and they successfully raise more than nine out of ten adopted chicks at least until fledging.

Another technique, known as hacking, introduces peregrine chicks into the wild without parent

Victim of habitat loss due to dams, the endangered Colorado squawfish—here captured for study and release—still survives in the Yampa River.

birds. The chicks are placed in a large cage-like box in a suitable habitat and supplied with food by unseen (so the chicks will not "imprint" on them as their parents) human attendants until the chicks fledge and are able to kill on their own. Ideally, these fledglings will remember their "birthplaces" and return a few years later to establish new aeries.

In a little more than a decade, these recovery efforts have produced a tenfold increase in the number of known occupied peregrine aeries in Dinosaur and have also been successful across the country, even in the man-made canyons of large cities.

However, the peregrine's future is far from secure. Around Dinosaur there is a constant pressure to control the Mormon cricket, a native wingless grasshopper whose periodic population explosions and mass migrations are perceived as a threat to rangelands—though studies show that the crickets mostly eat "undesirable" plants and other insects.

Pesticides are not used within the monument, and compliance with the Endangered Species Act forbids aerial spraying of them within ten miles of any known peregrine aerie. However, if the peregrines or their prey fly beyond that limited zone of protection, they may still be eating toxic meals. And of course many birds, peregrines and prey alike, fly south for the winter—most to Latin American countries where DDT is still used.

SUGGESTED READING

COLORADO NATIVE PLANT SOCIETY. *Rare Plants of Colorado.* Estes Park: Rocky Mountain Nature Association, 1989.

DE GOLIA, JACK. *Fire: The Story Behind A Force of Nature.* Las Vegas, Nevada: KC Publications, Inc., 1989.

MURRAY, JOHN A. *Wildlife in Peril: The endangered Mammals of Colorado.* Boulder: Roberts Rinehart, Inc., 1987.

WOODLING, JOHN. *Colorado's Little Fish: A Guide to the Minnows and Other Lesser Known Fishes in the State of Colorado.* Denver: Colorado Division of Wildlife, 1985.

*The Fremont people did not build large
"cliff dwellings" as did their southern neighbors,
they probably had a variety of
seasonal campsites, but their movements
were governed by the progress of their gardens.*

Before there was a Monument

NPS PHOTO BY DAVID WHITMAN

The Fremont people built numerous rock and mud cysts to store
*dried corn, beans, and other foods. Such caches may have been set
aside for winter, droughts, or return visits to seasonally-used sites.*

Compared to the vast span of time represented by the rocks, humans have been around for a mere blink of an eye. But like the landscape itself, much of the human story at Dinosaur has been shaped by water.

THE NATIVE PEOPLE

The oldest human artifacts yet found within Dinosaur National Monument are a few stone projectile points, estimated to be about 7,000 years old. Other points from outside the boundaries, however, suggest human occupation of this region as early as 10,000 years ago or more.

These early people (termed PaleoIndians by modern archaeologists) left only scant clues, essentially just stone tools and animal bones. Bones found on the Great Plains east of the Rockies tell us that the people there lived largely on the meat of the last great Ice Age mammals: horses, camels, giant bison, and mammoths. Remains of some of these animals have also been found nearer the Dinosaur area, but so far no human artifacts have been definitely associated with them.

JEFF GNASS

Large, elaborately decorated anthropomorphs,
*or human-like figures, typify Fremont rock art. Some
people suggest that this scene depicts the taking of
"trophy" heads or scalps, but no one knows.*

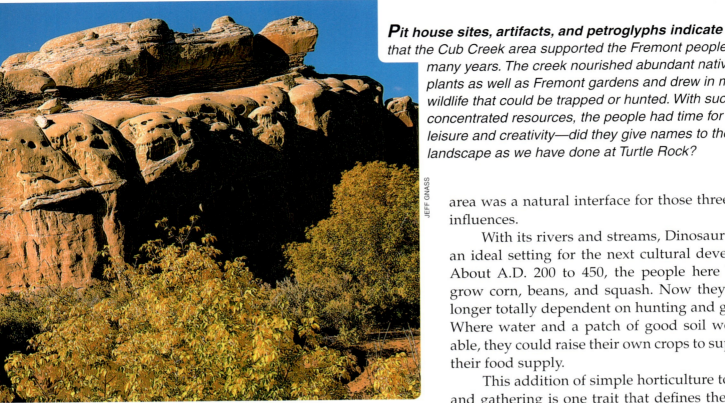

JEFF GNASS

Pit house sites, artifacts, and petroglyphs indicate that the Cub Creek area supported the Fremont people for many years. The creek nourished abundant native plants as well as Fremont gardens and drew in much wildlife that could be trapped or hunted. With such concentrated resources, the people had time for leisure and creativity—did they give names to the landscape as we have done at Turtle Rock?

As the larger species became extinct (and also as the climate became warmer and drier), the early hunters gradually turned to other game, ranging from modern bison and deer to rabbits, rodents, and birds. Introduction of the *atlatl*, a wooden spear-thrower that greatly increased the force of the throw, refined their hunting techniques.

The appearance of grinding stones (metates and manos) shows that they also relied more and more on wild plants for food. This transition from "big-game" hunting to a more varied hunting and gathering subsistence marks the beginning, about 6,500 years ago, of Archaic culture—a general lifestyle with many variations depending on time, region, and local resources.

In the monument, sites such as Deluge Shelter on Jones Hole Creek and Swelter Shelter near the Dinosaur Quarry preserve a lengthy record of human activity, from late PaleoIndian through Archaic and later. These rock-shelters were not permanent homes, but were repeatedly used as campsites by varied groups of hunter-gatherers.

These artifacts, especially projectile points, show similarities to those of the Great Basin to the west, the Plains to the north and east, and the Colorado and Uncompahgre plateaus to the south and east. Situated at the meeting of the Rocky Mountains and the Colorado Plateau, and with reliable water sources and a great diversity of habitats, the Dinosaur

area was a natural interface for those three cultural influences.

With its rivers and streams, Dinosaur was also an ideal setting for the next cultural development. About A.D. 200 to 450, the people here began to grow corn, beans, and squash. Now they were no longer totally dependent on hunting and gathering. Where water and a patch of good soil were available, they could raise their own crops to supplement their food supply.

This addition of simple horticulture to hunting and gathering is one trait that defines the Fremont Culture, so named for the Fremont River in southern Utah, where it was first studied. Archaeologists have since traced the culture through much of the eastern Great Basin and upper Colorado River drainage, which includes the Green and Yampa rivers. Like the earlier people, the Fremont interacted with surrounding cultures, adopting technologies (such as ceramics and the bow and arrow) that were instrumental in creating the "Fremont lifestyle".

The Fremont people did not build large "cliff dwellings" as did their southern neighbors the Anasazi, but that was because they had not completely abandoned a hunter-gatherer lifestyle. Like their ancestors, they probably had a variety of seasonal campsites, but their movements were governed by the progress of their gardens as well as the migration of animals and the maturing of native plants.

Occasionally the Fremont took shelter under natural overhangs, but more often they seem to have used those as storage areas (Mantle Cave, in Castle Park on the Yampa River, is a prime example), and built their own temporary houses on open ground. Along Cub Creek and Pool Creek they lived in small "villages" of pit houses, which were one-or two-room structures, sometimes dug into the ground, and roofed with hides or mud over a framework of wooden poles.

Whatever they lacked in enduring architecture, the Fremont made up for it with their artwork—another of their definitive traits and certainly the most visible evidence of them today. Their canvasses were

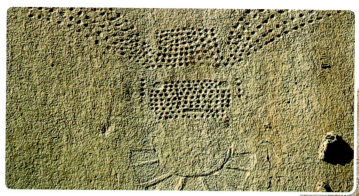

A *petroglyph near Echo Park shows both dot-pecked and fully-incised patterns in its design.*

F*remont artists used combinations of plants, minerals, and animal fat to make pigments for their rock art. Some designs combined both carving and painting, while others, like these pictographs in Jones Hole, were painted.*

PHOTOS BY JOHN P. GEORGE

WHAT *does* ROCK Art Mean?

nothing less than the cliff faces and canyon walls, preferably those having a smooth surface darkened by desert varnish, a natural deposit of mineral oxides and/or organic matter. By chipping or scratching through this veneer to expose the lighter sandstone beneath, the Fremont artists created durable drawings of animals, human figures (or perhaps deities or spirits), and abstract geometric designs.

There are whole galleries of this rock art in Castle Park, along Cub Creek, and at McKee Springs near Island Park, and smaller groups of them in Echo Park and many other locations. Most of the designs are petroglyphs, actually incised into the rock. Pictographs (drawings made by simply daubing natural pigments on lighter colored rock surfaces) are fairly rare, probably because they were more rapidly weathered away. A few have survived in protected spots such as the overhang of Deluge Shelter. Probably many designs originally included both carved and painted elements.

What does this rock art mean? Of the many possible interpretations—picture-writing, religious or ceremonial art, records of everyday life or unusual events, territorial boundary markers, glorified doodles—we cannot say which, if any, is correct. We can see that the makers must have spent considerable time and effort on it, and from this we can conclude that the Fremont people's lifestyle was a good step above mere subsistence. There was time to spend on self-expression as well as survival.

Yet their time as a distinct culture did eventually come to an end sometime around A.D. 1150 to 1300. It appears that the people reverted to a less-settled hunting and gathering life, possibly as their crops failed due to recurring droughts.

During this period they may also have been displaced and/or absorbed by Nomic speaking people who moved into the region from the west and south. These people are the ancestors of the Ute and Shoshone Indians who still live in the region today. The Utes and Shoshones originally lived by hunting and gathering; however, adoption of horses from the Spanish explorers in the seventeenth century gave them greater mobility, and they ranged over a wide area of western Colorado and eastern Utah. They probably hunted occasionally in parts of what is now Dinosaur National Monument but, in contrast to both earlier and later people, left little evidence of this passage.

Ashley wrote the first known description of Steamboat Rock: "a point of the mountain runs for a mile not wider than 50 or 100 [yards]... and the river runs immediately round it." The Yampa enters at left.

THE EXPLORERS

...and after going two leagues northwest [we] came to a large river which we named San Buenaventura...[The river flows] between two lofty stone hogbacks which, after forming a sort of corral, come so closely together that one can barely make out the gorge through which the river comes.

This, dated September 13, 1776, is the first written record of what is now Dinosaur National Monument. The writer was Fray Silvestre Velez de Escalante, one of a small party led by Fray Francisco Atanasio Dominquez. The two Franciscan fathers and their comrades were attempting to establish an overland route from Santa Fe, New Mexico, to the new missions in California.

Winter weather later turned them back, but here they camped beside the river for two days, then forded it and continued westward. The river was the one that we now call the Green River, and they crossed it about where it now leaves the monument near the Dinosaur Quarry. It would be another half-century before modern history again touched this area, but as before the encounter would take place along the Green River.

By the 1820s, a large chunk of the West had passed from Spanish to French to American hands, but Europe, by means of high fashion, still influenced the exploration of the region. A tall hat of beaver felt was *de rigueur* for the well-dressed gentleman. The thriving fur trade that grew out of the demand brought hundreds of trappers—the mountain men—to the banks of every river and stream from the Rockies to the Sierra Nevada.

The spring of 1825 found a party of such men, headed by William H. Ashley, camped beside the Shetkadee River north of the Uinta Mountains. They were primarily in search of beaver, but first they shot and skinned several buffalo, whose hides they stretched over a framework of willow branches to make a bullboat, a versatile frontier watercraft adapted from the Plains Indians.

After dividing most of this camp into overland exploring parties, Ashley climbed into the boat with the remaining six or seven men and set off down the river, expecting to find rich new trapping grounds along it. The river, variously known as the Shetka-dee, Shetskeedee, Seeds-ke-dee, and other corruptions of a Shoshone word meaning "prairie hen," was the one we now call the Green River.

The Ashley party was, as far as we know, the first group of people to descend the river through the canyons of Dinosaur. They found fewer beaver—and more rocks, rapids, and difficult portages—than they expected, and eventually abandoned the river downstream from the present monument area.

It seems likely that other mountain men would also have tried floating the Green River in search of beaver, but only one seems to have left any record of such journeys. Denis Julien, a little-known but well-traveled trapper, carved his name or initials on several canyon walls—in places accessible only from the water—along both the Green and the Colorado, with dates ranging from 1831 to 1838. The latter date appears on a cliff in Whirlpool Canyon in Dinosaur.

By that time trappers were finding slim pickings, for they had all but wiped out the West's beaver population, and when changing fashions made silk hats the new rage of the 1840s, the fur trade quietly died. However, the mountain men had pioneered the routes along which the great waves of westward migration were now sweeping toward California and Oregon. These were overland trails, crossing the Continental Divide over the gentle grade of South Pass, and giving the rugged canyons and wild rivers of Dinosaur a wide berth.

Thus, when John Wesley Powell set out to explore the Green and Colorado rivers in 1869, his knowledge of geology was more helpful to him than any historical records then available. He had heard of Ashley, but what he had heard was inaccurate and hardly reassuring:

> ...an old-time mountaineer once told me about a party of men starting down the [Green] river and Ashley was named as one. The story runs that the boat was swamped and some of the party drowned in one of the canyons below.

Even worse were the rumors of waterfalls higher than Niagara, and furious whirlpools or "sucks" that would swallow any boat, and even places where the rivers tunneled underground. But Powell reasoned that such large, swift, silt-laden rivers ought to have abraded their beds to a more even profile, with rapids, to be sure, but probably not impassable waterfalls or underground channels.

Fortunately, Powell's logic was correct, but the names his men gave to some of the rapids—such as Disaster Falls and Hell's Half Mile in the Canyon of Lodore—show that even without a Niagara, passage down the river was no simple matter. Indeed, both this expedition and Powell's second one in 1871-72

JOHN P. GEORGE

The Dominguez-Escalante party found the Green River shallow enough to ford near this site; the Ashley and Powell expeditions found its quiet flow a relief after the wild ride through Split Mountain Gorge.

Pat Lynch, the "hermit of Echo Park," posed jauntily
for Ellsworth and Emery Kolb when they floated the Green
River in 1911. The Kolbs' photographs showed the remote
canyon country to many people—some of whom would later
defend the scenery and solitude that Pat had loved.

those hardy, independent people who did stake their claims to a livelihood in the canyons.

SETTLERS, HERMITS, AND OUTLAWS

Though the Green and Yampa rivers carry plenty of water, getting to it is another matter. The high canyon walls that make such great scenery also limit access to the rivers, so most settlement in the Dinosaur area took place outside the main canyons.

Browns Park, the relatively open valley above the Gates of Lodore, had long been used by various Indian groups, especially as a winter camp because of its mild climate. A few Texas cattle herds on their way to the California gold fields also wintered there, and after the Civil War, a number of families established homes and ranches in the valley. A similar small ranching community developed in Deerlodge and Lily parks on the Yampa River, just before it plunges into its deep, narrow canyon through the monument.

probably portaged as great a distance as they actually floated.

Powell's self-designed boats, most of them built of oak and each equipped with two pairs of oars plus a long rudder-like sweep oar at the stern proved to be too heavy and hard to maneuver through most of the rapids. Disaster Falls, which smashed one of the boats to pieces, proved that oak was no match for the force of water against rock.

Powell's explorations put most of the canyon country's names on the map and were pioneer efforts in documenting the diverse geology, natural history, and Indian cultures of the region. More significantly for the future, Powell was one of the few people of his time to recognize the greatest obstacle to extensive settlement and development of the West—its aridity.

Powell foresaw that serious agriculture would require cooperative irrigation development, quite in contrast to the tradition of the independent homesteaders who had claimed the moister lands to the east. Ultimately such development awaited federal action, but in the meantime, there were a few of

A few families, though, ventured farther into the canyons, finding the rare places where the walls drew back enough to provide some bottomland on which to build a house and grow a few crops. These included the Ruples in Island Park on the Green River, the Chews on Pool Creek near Echo Park, and the Mantles in Castle Park. These settlers actually utilized (and altered) much more land than the small plots on which they lived, for they also raised cattle or sheep, which required vast areas of the adjacent benchlands and plateaus for grazing.

Some people, such as Pat Lynch, seemed to crave the solitude the canyons offered. A former soldier and sailor, Pat wandered into Echo Park in the 1870s and stayed for nearly 40 years. He raised a few cows and horses but mostly lived off the land, with a little help from his military pension and a little freeloading off the other settlers.

Since human company was rare, he talked to himself, to "spirits," and to a mountain lion who shared his domain. Pat claimed that the big cat answered him, too, in a voice sweeter than Jenny Lind's (a famous singer of the time). Today, Jenny Lind

Rock repeats the echoes off Steamboat Rock, and Echo Park itself is commonly known as Pat's Hole.

Still others found the canyons' remoteness an occasional asset. One of these was a ranch hand names Charley Jones. Thinking he had killed a man in a fight, Charley fled to a deep tributary canyon of the Green River and lay low for a winter. Some accounts claim that John Wesley Powell had already named the canyon for Stephen Vandiver Jones, a member of his second expedition, but local folks say the name "Jones Hole" really originated when Charley "holed up" there. He came out when he learned that his supposed victim had lived.

Local tradition has it that genuine outlaws such as Butch Cassidy, the Sundance Kid, and others also hid out in the canyons at times. Browns Park was a fairly well-known outlaw hangout at the turn of the century. One of several branches of the "Outlaw Trail" led from there down along the east side of the Canyon of Lodore, across the Yampa, and southward to the Robbers Roost country of southern Utah.

Naturally, though, Butch and his cohorts didn't often say much about their whereabouts or travels. Toward the turn of the century, the Dinosaur canyon country was still not much better known, except to those hardy few settlers and cowhands, than when Dominguez and Escalante first brushed its edges. That would finally change as some people began to look at the rivers in new ways—some of which could also change the rivers themselves.

The primitive road into Echo Park passes the Pool Creek Ranch, where Jack and Mary Chew made their home in 1910. Now part of the monument, the ranch is preserved as a remnant of pioneer history.

THE FATE OF THE RIVERS

As John Wesley Powell had pointed out, in the arid West the most valuable resource is water itself, and most of the limited supply of it is in the Colorado River system. If this water was to be fully utilized for agriculture, cities, and power generation, the rivers would have to be controlled. In 1909 engineers

Quiet evening shadows and reflections in Echo Park give no hint of the storm of controversy that once centered on this spot. In the 1950s the Bureau of Reclamation proposed to build a dam just downstream. The impounded waters of the Green and Yampa rivers would have risen almost to the canyon rims here, but resounding protests from across the nation stopped the plans.

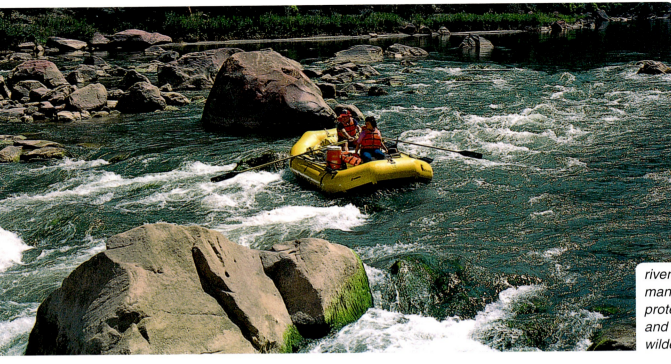

With their ability to bounce off rocks, inflatable rafts helped make river running a little easier—and so popular that river use is now carefully managed in order to protect canyon ecosystems and preserve a sense of wilderness.

drilled into the canyon floor at the Gates of Lodore to test its suitability to anchor a dam, but they failed to find firm bedrock.

In the ensuing years, however, power companies and government agencies identified more than a dozen potential dam sites along the Green River, and several on the Yampa as well. No immediate construction followed these surveys, and in the meantime other events began to shift the fate of the rivers.

While the dam surveyors were busy drilling at the Gates of Lodore, a small party of boaters drifted past them. Organized by Julius F. Stone, a wealthy industrialist, and guided by Nathaniel Galloway, a trapper from nearby Vernal, Utah, this group was floating the river not in search of furs or scientific discovery, but for the sheer fun and adventure of it.

Galloway had already boated the canyons numerous times and is credited with the innovation that revolutionized river running: in rapids, he turned his lightweight, broad-beamed boats around and faced downstream, rowing at an angle to the current to pivot around rocks, straightening out to meet the waves. Instead of trying to out-muscle the river as Powell had done, he outmaneuvered it.

Following this example, a small but slowly growing number of other people began to float the rivers, both the Green and the Yampa, and most emerged with glowing tales, photographs, and even movies of the scenic splendors of the canyons. Further, by the mid-1930s several thousand people visited Dinosaur National Monument, then just the quarry site, each year. Many of them also braved the

rough dirt road down to the mouth of Split Mountain Gorge for a picnic or just for the view.

Observing these trends, the National Park Service began to take an interest in the lands beyond the quarry, and made several studies of the possible creation of a new national park or monument, or simply an expansion of the existing monument.

The latter proved to be the most expedient course, and on July 14, 1938, President Franklin D. Roosevelt issued a proclamation enlarging Dinosaur National Monument to 325 square miles, including nearly 100 miles to the Green and Yampa rivers. The scenic canyons were now protected—or were they?

In 1950, the U.S. Bureau of Reclamation released its report on the Colorado River Storage Project, a comprehensive plan involving ten dams and reservoirs in five states. Two of the proposed impoundments lay within the expanded Dinosaur National Monument.

One dam was to be located just inside the mouth of Split Mountain Gorge, and would back water up through that canyon, Island Park and Whirlpool Canyon, virtually to the foot of the other dam. The other, known as the Echo Park Dam and designed to be the second largest in the entire project, would pool water for the whole length of the Canyon of Lodore and most of the Yampa Canyon as well. In short, all of the canyons in the monument would be wholly or partially filled by reservoirs.

The project's supporters correctly anticipated that there might be some objection to this tampering with the scenery, but the reaction from outdoor clubs and conservation organizations went far beyond anticipations. The real issue to these groups was nothing less than the future of the whole National Park System. Allowing dams in Dinosaur would set a dangerous precedent that could open any national park or monument to inappropriate development.

Ultimately this outcry changed a regional issue into a national one, and the debate raged through the Department of the Interior and into Congress. When it became apparent that insistence on the Echo Park Dam could jeopardize the entire project, its supporters grudgingly backed down. In 1956, Congress authorized construction of four of the proposed dams, but Echo Park and Split Mountain were not among them. Dinosaur National Monument would remain untouched by dams.

But actually it did not. One of the four approved dams was Flaming Gorge, at a site on the Green River about 45 miles upstream from the Gates of Lodore. A little more than three years after the project was authorized, the Green was diverted into a tunnel and the dam began rising from the canyon floor. As the last bucket of concrete topped off the dam in 1962, the new reservoir was backing up behind it.

A river emerges from the base of Flaming Gorge Dam but it is not the same Green River that once was. Drawn from the depths of the reservoir, the water is chilled, and it has left its load of mud and silt behind the dam. The peak spring runoffs are captured in the reservoir and released gradually over the rest of the year. The river still rises and falls, but daily, in response to electrical power demands.

These effects of the dam are felt down the Green, into Dinosaur National Monument and beyond. Recreational boaters lament the loss of the "big water" that Ashley and Powell saw, but this is only one of the more obvious changes. More subtle but pervasive effects include dense riverbank thickets that are no longer scoured out by spring floods; erosion of beaches and sandbars that are no longer rebuilt by new sediments; loss of backwater "fish nursery" areas; changes in the water's dissolved oxygen content; and so on. As we will later see, all of these changes have in turn profoundly affected much of the native life in and along the river.

In contrast to the Green, the Yampa River is still "untamed" by major dams. To boaters this means challenges and thrills, when spring runoff turns the Yampa into thick brown flood thundering through Tepee, Big Joe, and Warm Springs rapids. But the wild Yampa is far more than a recreational resource. Its natural floods and trickles, its mud and sand and cobbles, and the plants and animals that live in it and on its banks—all of these are part of the last

JEFF GNASS

The Weber Sand-stone produces some of Dinosaur's most striking scenery. Ancient winds once sculpted its sands into vast dune fields; now the Yampa River carves a sinuous maze through it.

largely-natural river ecosystem in the entire Colorado River drainage.

But only the last 46 miles of the Yampa River are protected within Dinosaur National Monument. A large dam on the Yampa outside the monument would still irrevocably alter the river ecosystem, just as Flaming Gorge Dam has changed the Green. Thus the Yampa presents us with another kind of challenge: to apply the preservation philosophy of a national monument outside its boundaries as well as within them. It is not just a matter or providing white water recreation or protecting scenic vistas. It is a matter of preserving a unique and irreplaceable diversity of land, water, and life—a richly woven fabric in which we humans are just one thread.

SUGGESTED READING

CASSELS, E. STEVEN. *The Archaeology of Colorado*. Boulder: Johnson Books, 1983.

CHAVEZ, FRAY ANGELICO, AND TED J. WARNER. *The Dominguez-Escalante Journal*. Provo, Utah: Brigham Young University Press, 1976.

MARTINEAU, LAVAN. *The Rocks Begin to Speak*. Las Vegas, Nevada: KC Publications, 1973.

POWELL, JOHN WESLEY. *The Exploration of the Colorado River and Its Canyons*. New York: Dover Publications, 1961. (Originally published as *Canyons of the Colorado*, 1895.)

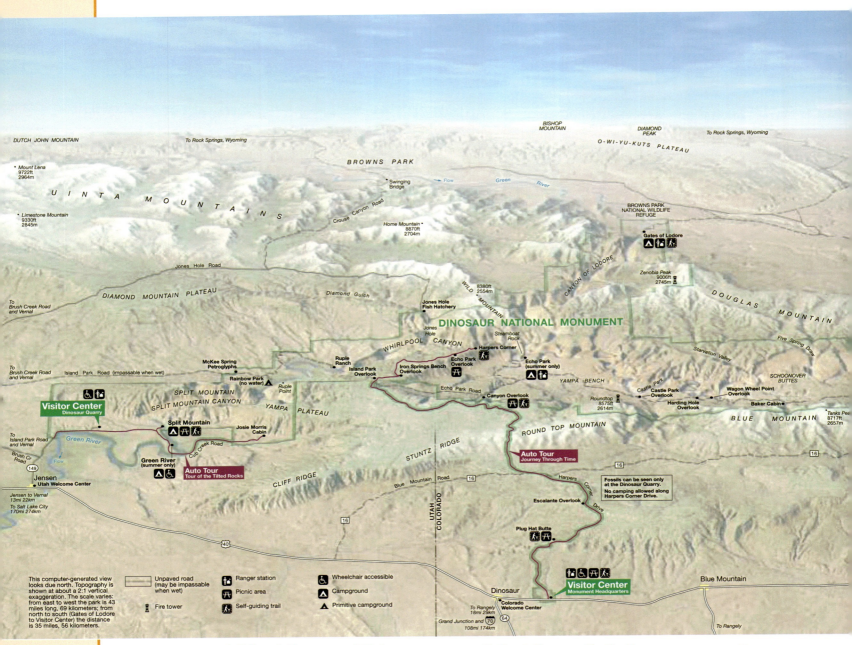

This computer-generated view looks due north. Topography is shown at about a 2:1 vertical exaggeration. The scale varies: from east to west the park is 43 miles long, 69 kilometers; from north to south (Gates of Lodore to Visitor Center) the distance is 35 miles, 56 kilometers.

Unpaved road (may be impassable when wet)

Ranger station

Picnic area

Fire tower

Wheelchair accessible

Campground

Self-guiding trail

Primitive campground

All About Dinosaur National Monument

Contact Us

Dinosaur National Monument
4545 East Highway 40
Dinosaur, CO 81610-9724

By Phone
(970) 374-3000

Website
www.nps.gov/dino

Intermountain Natural History Association (INHA) is a partner with public lands management agencies working to preserve our shared national heritage. It is the source for books, maps, posters, videos and gift items pertaining to a remarkable region of our country. Profits from all sales are donated back to their partners to help with scientific, educational and interpretive efforts of those agencies. Visit their web site at: www.inhaweb.com.

Junior Ranger

To become a Junior Ranger, children are given a booklet and complete a number of activities about Dinosaur National Monument. Upon completion, you will be awarded a paleontoloist badge. Wear it with pride!

A Fragile Legacy

By itself, Dinosaur National Monument cannot guarantee the future of the endangered species that live within or pass through it. Pesticides in food chains, the downstream effects of dams, air pollution from nearby power plants or distant cities, and other threats (such as crude oil that spilled into the Yampa River from a broken pipeline in June, 1989) do not stop at the monument boundaries. Conservationists used to speak of "setting aside" our national parks and monuments to protect them from misuse or harmful development, but in the long run there is no "aside."

Some people may say "So what?"—that if peregrine falcons or bonytail chubs cannot adapt to a changing world, their eventual extinction will be no different from that of the countless other species that have become extinct in the past. No doubt some would question the costs and merits of intensive recovery efforts. And some would say that human needs must take precedence over those of any other species.

But there are also people who can offer many counterarguments. They will point out that man-made changes are often so rapid that a species has no chance to adapt as it would to natural change. They may feel that if we are the cause of a species' decline, we have a moral obligation to try to reverse it. They can list many species that have scientific, medical, economic, or simply aesthetic value for us.

Contact Us

Intermountain Natural History Association
1291 E. Highway 40
Vernal, UT 84078-2830

By Phone
(800) 845-3466

And they will state that species diversity is a measure of the Earth's overall health and that a planet becoming increasingly unfit for wildlife will eventually become unfit for human life.

Dinosaur National Monument cannot dictate how we will resolve these conflicting viewpoints, but it can give us a rare perspective on the questions and choices they pose. We can survey a vast span of time in Dinosaur's rocks, and perhaps feel some much-needed humility at our own very recent arrival on the scene. We can study the adaptations of many kinds of life, including human, to Dinosaur's past and present environments. We can compare a natural river to a controlled one and measure the ecological, as well as economic, costs and benefits of the changes.

In the Dinosaur Quarry, we may mourn the passing of the dinosaurs, but we can also thank the farsighted people who strove to preserve their remains. Our descendants may mourn the loss of today's living species, wild places, and free-flowing rivers. But perhaps, in Dinosaur National Monument, they will thank us for being farsighted enough to preserve some of them.

C. ALLAN MORGAN

When these youngsters are grown, will today's wildlife be only museum specimens like dinosaurs? Perhaps not, if we preserve places like Dinosaur National Monument.

KC Publications has been the leading publisher of colorful, interpretive books about National Park areas, public lands, Indian lands, and related subjects for over 45 years. We have 5 active series—over 125 titles—with Translation Packages in up to 8 languages for over half the areas we cover. Write, call, or visit our web site for our full-color catalog.

Our series are:

The Story Behind the Scenery® – Compelling stories of over 65 National Park areas and similar Public Land areas. Some with Translation Packages.

in pictures... Nature's Continuing Story® – A companion, pictorially oriented, series on America's National Parks. All titles have Translation Packages.

For Young Adventurers® – Dedicated to young seekers and keepers of all things wild and sacred. Explore America's Heritage from A to Z.

Voyage of Discovery® – Exploration of the expansion of the western United States.

Indian Culture and the Southwest – All about Native Americans, past and present.

To receive our full-color catalog featuring over 125 titles—Books and other related specialty products:
Call (800) 626-9673, fax (928) 684-5189, write to the address below, or visit our web sites at www.kcpublications.com

Published by KC Publications, P.O. Box 3615, Wickenburg, AZ 85358

Inside Back Cover:
The Yampa River carved its own history, but its future is in our hands.
Photo by Jeff Gnass.

Back Cover:
Returning sandstone to sand, erosion sculpts Split Mountain's crest.
Photo by Jeff Gnass.

Created, Designed, and Published in the U.S.A.
Printed by Tien Wah Press (Pte.) Ltd, Singapore
Pre-Press by United Graphic Pte. Ltd